BIBLICAL LITERACY *FOR* KIDS

TEACHING STUDENTS TO READ THE BIBLE FOR THEMSELVES

BIBLICAL LITERACY

FOR

KIDS

TEACHING STUDENTS
TO READ THE BIBLE
FOR THEMSELVES

MANDY KNOWLTON

HIGH BRIDGE
BOOKS & MEDIA

Contents

No part of this book was written by artificial intelligence.

Find companion guides, download graphics, and connect with the author by visiting
www.biblicalliteracyforkids.com.

Introduction

I F I COULD GIVE ONE THING TO THE KIDS IN YOUR LIFE, IT would be the gift of biblical literacy. Why? Because biblical literacy is the key to growing in Christ, and I believe that a lack of biblical literacy is one of the most pressing issues facing the Church today.

Simply put, **biblical literacy is the ability to independently read, understand, and apply a Bible passage to your life.** These skills may sound easy, but teaching them can be difficult without a guide. This book is designed to be your roadmap for biblical literacy instruction, whether you are a parent, grandparent, teacher, or ministry leader. Any adult can help kids grow in biblical literacy.

Students are ready for the material in this book once they are tackling beginner chapter books (the ones that still have a few pictures) and understanding those books well. Most kids reach this level in about third grade, when they are eight or nine years old, but some children arrive earlier or later. As a result, most of my examples and sample lessons are from students in grades three through six.

If your student has not yet reached the appropriate level of reading independence, you may certainly still use this book to begin modeling some of the strategies as you read the Bible together. However, do not expect students to fully grasp these skills until they begin reading those longer texts.

Perhaps your student is much older, maybe a high schooler or even a young adult. You can also use this book's strategies for those age groups; in fact, you will find that they will acquire the skills you are teaching even faster than the younger students because they have more experience with other literacy tasks.

While this book mainly focuses on kids, no one is ever too old to begin the journey of biblical literacy – not even adults! You could easily adapt this book's strategies for an adult study group, perhaps one for parents who want to read the Bible with their children. You could also practice using these strategies yourself to improve your own comprehension. Regardless of which age group you are teaching, consistent practice of biblical literacy skills will yield valuable results.

You may notice that this book is rather short. I have purposefully designed it to be a quick and easy read so that you can get on with the important business of teaching students. Every person I know who works with children has limited time in their schedules for reading, and I am sure that you are no different. It is my prayer that this brief guide will facilitate spiritual growth for both you and your students. May the Lord richly bless you as you share His Word with others!

1

The Case for Biblical Literacy Instruction

WHO TAUGHT YOU TO READ THE BIBLE? WAS IT A PARent, a ministry leader, or a teacher? If you are like many of the Christian adults I know, the answer is probably, "No one."

Now, I'm not saying that you didn't receive admonishment about the importance of reading the Bible when you attended church. Most pastors do a wonderful job of explaining that their members should be reading the Bible. Many churches provide reading plans, devotionals, and tips on how to have the perfect "quiet time." Adults may even meet together to study the Bible. All of these activities are great, but something is missing – and for most, what is missing is personal instruction in biblical literacy skills. After all, encouraging someone to read the Bible is not the same as actually teaching them how to do it.

Biblical literacy is the ability to independently read, understand, and apply a Bible passage to your life. If you can read a passage of the Bible, understand its meaning, and apply it to your life *without an accompanying sermon or study guide,* then you have biblical literacy. These skills of reading, understanding, and applying must be directly taught in order for people to master them.

For most adults I know, this type of direct teaching has never happened. Literacy competence is assumed, so most churches have never devoted themselves to teaching specific reading skills. Perhaps this approach worked in the past, but the need for precise instruction in biblical literacy is very necessary today. This book will equip you to address this pressing need.

I believe most adults would be willing to teach others how to read the Bible if they were more secure in their own ability to interpret the text. But many lack confidence in their understanding of the Bible, much less its application to their daily lives.

Consider this familiar scenario: during an adult Bible study class, a group member reads a selected biblical text aloud. The study leader asks some simple questions about the basic meaning of the text and receives a smattering of responses. But then the leader asks, "How can we apply this text to our lives?" The room grows uncomfortably silent until that one person pipes up with the answer. This person seems to always be able to answer those application questions! The leader may feel frustrated because he can never get anyone else to answer and the rest of the class really isn't growing in biblical literacy. Instead, they have trained themselves to simply wait for that one person's answer since that person seems to have all of the answers anyway.

I would argue that the "constant answerer" in that scenario is not necessarily spiritually superior to the others in the class. Most likely, he or she has a high level of literacy skills and has intuitively applied them to the biblical text. But each member of the class could be taught to do the same with proper instruction. Then everyone would be able to apply the truths of the Bible to their own lives.

Today, we have an unprecedented array of biblical resources. In English-speaking countries, access to the Bible – in any version you wish – is at our fingertips constantly thanks to the internet and an abundance of printed materials. We have a plentiful supply of study Bibles, commentaries, handbooks, and devotionals. But access to resources is useless if literacy skills are low, and indeed, they are problematic. I have witnessed the decline in general reading competency firsthand with my students over my past 17 years of teaching, watching as more and more kids arrive at school unprepared for the rigors of truly comprehending text well.

Our U.S. national test scores paint a stark picture: in 2022, only 33% of fourth graders scored at or above the reading proficiency standard on the National Assessment of Educational Progress (NAEP) test. In the same year, 31% of eighth graders were at or above proficiency. Only 37% of high school seniors were at or above proficiency in 2019, which is the most recent test for that grade level.[1]

Clearly, we have a problem with literacy in this country. And because the Bible is such a complex text, it actually requires more advanced reading skills to truly understand and apply it to our lives. Simple reading "proficiency" will not do. The test scores above reveal that more students than ever are arriving at church without the skills they need to successfully read the Bible on their own.

So what can be done? This book is designed to help parents, educators, and other concerned adults teach biblical literacy skills with confidence. Together, we will examine effective reading strategies in a detailed, comprehensible way. I will show you how these general reading skills apply to the biblical text and describe the order in which they should be taught, including practical lesson examples and tips on how to put the whole process together. I will also explain how to connect to your students in a relational way so that they can learn from you. This book is designed to be accessible to all, regardless of previous educational experience.

Biblical Literacy's Impact on Students

What happens to students when they are taught to read the Bible? In 2022, Barna Group published *The Open Generation*, a research study of nearly 25,000 teens from around the world that captured their views on Jesus, the Bible, and justice. Barna used several questions to determine the teens' attitudes toward the Bible, defining Bible-engaged teens as those who believe it is the Word of God and read it several times per week. The data makes it clear that time spent studying the Bible instills a Christian worldview: the research-ers found that among Bible-engaged teens, 84% believe the Bible teaches them about their purpose in life, and 80% believe it shows them how to live wisely in today's society.[2] This is great news! But the problem was that only 8% of the teens could be considered Bible-engaged.[3]

Yes, you read that right: only 8% of nearly 25,000 teens were considered Bible-engaged. That means 92% of those teens, for vari-ous reasons, do not consistently look to God's Word to guide their lives.

There is hope, however; the same study found that 56% of Bible-engaged teens received help in studying the Bible from a parent or guardian. Bible-engaged teens also listed pastors, Bible study lead-ers, and Sunday School teachers as contributors to their understand-ing of the Bible.[4] In other words, all adults can positively affect a student's connection with God's Word in meaningful ways.

A biblical worldview is essential to students' spiritual survival. In today's world of increasing evil, many are unashamed of their sin – in fact, they wouldn't even recognize that there *is* sin! Our society is constantly redefining what it means to be "good" or "successful." The constant pressure of social media, the rise of online-only inter-actions, the normalization of violent content, and the increasing promiscuity of our world put young people on dangerous ground. What can safeguard students' hearts against the ever-present pull of the world's way of thinking? An important part of the answer is a solid foundation in biblical literacy skills because this will greatly aid students in their understanding of both God and the world. Keep reading to see how you can play a pivotal role in giving the gift of biblical literacy to young people.

---

[1] U.S. Department of Education. Institute of Education Sciences, National Cen-ter for Education Statistics, National Assessment of Educational Progress (NAEP), 2022 Reading Assessment.

[2] Barna Group. October 5, 2022. "Global Teens Share Their Perceptions of Jesus, the Bible & Justice." Accessed September 30, 2024. https://www.barna.com/research/open-generation-perceptions/.

[3] Barna Group. 2022. "Explore the Data." Accessed September 30, 2024. https://www.barna.com/the-open-generation/explore-the-data/.

[4] Hartman, Nick. October 26, 2022. "A Reflection on Barna's Open Generation Report." Accessed September 30, 2024. https://www.youthpastortheologian.com/blog/a-reflection-on-barnas-open-generation-report.

2

Teaching Like Jesus

HAVE YOU EVER STOPPED TO CONSIDER WHY JESUS WAS such an effective teacher? For a long time, I had never really thought about this. Like so many others, I spent my time studying *what* He taught, not *how* He taught it. Besides, since Jesus is fully God, it seemed obvious that He would be successful. But then I reflected on Jesus' humanity – how He willingly accepted the limitations of being a man. So during His time on Earth, He would have needed to do things like get people's attention, raise His voice to be heard, and relate to others. And yet, despite these limitations, He was the greatest teacher of all time. How was He so successful?

As you begin the important endeavor of teaching biblical literacy skills, it can be tempting to jump straight into *what* you will be teaching: those reading strategies that are so crucial to helping students learn. However, *how* you teach is just as important as *what* you teach. So let's examine the success of Jesus' ministry to see what we can learn for our work with young people.

Incarnation Ambassadors: The Importance of Relationships

The very first thing we must notice is that Jesus began His earthly ministry with the incarnation. The incarnation was a relational act; God was no longer distant but came near to His creation in the person of Jesus. Through Christ, God showed the world that He desired a personal relationship with each person.

We see the importance of relationships during Jesus' entire ministry: He walked and talked with His disciples, touched lepers, welcomed children, and spent time with the outcasts. He was not simply there to impart information; He was there to embody God's personal, loving relationship.

In 2 Corinthians 5, Paul explains that we, as Christians, have been given the ministry of reconciliation – of bringing people back into a right relationship with God. In verse 20 of that same chapter, Paul explains, "We are therefore Christ's ambassadors, as though God were making his appeal through us." As an ambassador of Jesus, you have the privilege of being God's representative to the students you work with. Your life is a window through which your students can see their Creator. You're not just teaching them reading strategies; you're helping them develop a relationship with God.

What does this mean practically during biblical literacy time? For one thing, you cannot simply be a dispenser of information. You have to make time to learn more about your students' lives and appropriately share with them about your own. The reading strategies you will be teaching will help students connect the biblical text to their own lives, but you cannot possibly hope to facilitate that process if you do not know your students. Therefore, you must strive to model His care, compassion, and grace when you work with them, especially when they ask questions, struggle, or misbehave. You must also make time for relationships to grow.

Motivation Matters

While Jesus' loving care was available to everyone, He was discerning about who He chose to invest time in. When He called His disciples, He expected them to give up jobs, home, family, and security. In fact, when a teacher of the law asked to follow Jesus, He didn't sugarcoat the truth: "Foxes have dens and birds have nests, but the Son of Man has no place to lay his head" (Matt. 8:20). Jesus was looking for motivated followers who were willing to sacrifice for growth.

But He wasn't just asking them to give things up for no reason. He was calling them to something greater.

In the same way, as Christ's ambassador, you must be wise about how you invest your time. You are looking for motivated students or, at the very least, students who can be motivated. It cannot be overstated enough that students must be invested in the process of building biblical literacy. They have to want to learn it because the steps of real thinking about the text take both time and focus.

In today's world of limited attention spans and instant answers, it is highly likely that most kids have never been required to give that much thought to what they are reading. It is commonplace in schools now to hear phrases like, "I don't need to know it; I'll just ask AI!" or "I didn't read the book; I just read the online summary. Good enough!" Many students still get good grades with so little effort.

So most of your students are unlikely to show up automatically excited about learning something that requires actual effort. You are asking them to experience the discomfort of real learning, which is a sacrifice these days. This is when you use Jesus' strategy: you must call them to something greater.

Can you concisely articulate why your students should bother growing in biblical literacy? A clear vision statement is important, and it may change slightly based on who you are teaching. For example, when I was teaching Bible lessons to my fifth graders, I would always say, "God always has something to say to you; you just need to stick around long enough to figure out what it is!" In fact, I said it so often that soon I could just start the phrase and they would all finish it for me! That particular vision statement worked for those students because they were always very concerned about being "in the know," so the statement focused our time on something that mattered to them.

Now, however, I have a different vision statement for the third-grade student I am teaching. Hers is, "Learning to read the Bible for yourself will help you grow to be more like Jesus." This vision statement works for her because she is already a Christian and cares about becoming more Christlike. She is also quite motivated by anything that makes her more independent, which is why her vision statement includes an emphasis on reading the Bible for herself.

A clear vision statement is motivating, but, like with my third grader, a clear and individualized vision statement is even more powerful. So what sort of vision statement will be most impactful for your students? What already motivates them? Let's take a look at some possible characteristics of students and their matching vision statements.

Vision Statement	Possible Student Characteristics
Learning to read the Bible can help you find God's answers to tough questions.	Students questioning injustice or evil in the world.
God's truth doesn't change, and it's available to you if you look for it.	Students who are facing uncertainty, anxiety, or are bothered by the pace of change in the world.
Let's find out how God's Word is always relevant to your life.	Students who have been in church for a long time, know all of the basic Bible stories, and need to move beyond simple "Sunday School" answers. They will be curious about how the Bible is *always* relevant.
God always has something to say to you; you just need to stick around long enough to figure out what it is!	Students who feel left out when they aren't "in the know." For these kids, God speaking to them is intriguing.
Learning to read the Bible for yourself will help you become more like Jesus.	Students who desire to grow in healthy independence, who are already Christians and have

	demonstrated a desire to "level up" in their spiritual maturity.

Notice that none of these vision statements are about changing the Bible to be something it's not. Rather, they are about connecting with the students where they are and moving them closer to Jesus. Pray and ask the Holy Spirit to guide you to the best vision statement for your kids.

Conversation and Questions

Another important aspect of Jesus' teaching is how He presented information to those around Him. Sometimes He was very direct, but often He preached in parables and engaged people in conversations. For example, consider the issue of Jesus' identity. We learn in Luke 9:18-21 that the crowds couldn't decide who Jesus was. Some people said he was John the Baptist, others thought he was Elijah, and some believed He was another prophet from the past. When Peter declared that Jesus is God's Messiah, the Bible says that "Jesus strictly warned [the disciples] not to tell this to anyone" (Luke 9:21). Why doesn't Jesus just tell the people who He is? Why is He content to let people stay in confusion? Wouldn't it have been much simpler to be more direct about something so important?

Yes, it would have been simpler, but Jesus was not after a basic understanding. He wanted people to look for clues, listen to Him closely, ask lots of questions, and wrestle with His ideas. He knew that cognitive struggle is beneficial – even necessary – for growth. So He did not usually provide easy answers.

You will face the same problem when you are taking your students through Bible passages. Some sections will be difficult, and it will be tempting to just give your students the answer and do all of the thinking for them. Don't do it! Instead, make them think, help them make connections – this is how they grow. This approach takes longer, but it's well worth it. Realistically, there will be times when you will need to explain something directly, but make sure you are still forcing your students to do most of the thinking.

Let's examine Matthew 8:18-22 to see the conversational teaching method in action.

> When Jesus saw the crowd around him, he gave orders to cross to the other side of the lake. Then a teacher of the law came to him and said, "Teacher, I will follow you wherever you go."
>
> Jesus replied, "Foxes have dens and birds have nests, but the Son of Man has no place to lay his head."
>
> Another disciple said to him, "Lord, first let me go and bury my father."
>
> But Jesus told him, "Follow me, and let the dead bury their own dead."

Here's part of an example conversation:

Adult: I'm wondering about something. Is Jesus turning away people who want to follow Him?

Student: It seems like it.

Adult: Why would He do that?

Student: Uh… *[Blank stare]*

At this point, you might be tempted to rush in and give the student the answer. After all, blank stares and silence can be uncomfortable. But don't do it! Push your students to think with more questions.

Adult: Hmm…what does Jesus say to the Teacher of the Law?

Student: "Foxes have dens and birds have nests, but the Son of Man has no place to lay his head."

Adult: Right. What does that mean?

Student: I don't know.

Adult: Well, what is the same about dens and nests?

Student: Oh! Those are the animals' homes!

Adult: Right! So why bring that up? Read that section again.

Student: *[Rereads]* Oh! He's saying that He has no home!

Adult: Yes! Why does that matter to the Teacher of the Law?

Student: Well, he probably doesn't want to be homeless.

Adult: You got it! Okay, but what about the other guy? It seems really harsh that Jesus won't let him bury his dad, doesn't it?

Student: Well, yeah.

Adult: So why does He say it?

Student: *[Blank stare]*

The last time the adult got the blank stare, she just needed to push her students to think more. This time, however, the adult does need to tell the students directly some important background information about the culture during Jesus' time. Students are unlikely to know this information on their own and will not understand the passage without it. But the adult will only provide the necessary facts and then resume questioning.

Adult: Something you should know is that in Jesus' time, a person had to be buried right away after death. Otherwise, the body would start to stink! So as soon as someone died, the family would be totally focused on the funeral preparations and burial. Does that make sense?

Student: Yes.

Adult: So *where* did Jesus meet the guy who wants to wait to bury his father?

Student: In a crowd.

Adult: Is this man busy planning a funeral or burial?

Student: No…

Adult: So what does that tell you about this guy's father?

Student: Uh…

Adult: Is the father dead yet?

Student: Oh my gosh! No, he's probably not!

Adult: How do you know?

Student: Because the man is out wandering around in a crowd, not planning a funeral.

Adult: Right. If his father was dead, this man would be very busy with his family. So why would this man ask to bury his father?

Student: I don't know.

Adult: Well, how long will it take for his father to die?

Student: I don't know. Nobody would know that except God.

Adult: Exactly! So does this guy actually want to follow Jesus?

Student: No, it doesn't seem like it.

Adult: How do you know?

Student: Because it seems like he's just making up excuses that sound good so that he doesn't have to go with Jesus.

This discussion took way longer than it would have if the adult had just told the students the answers when they got stuck. However, cognitive struggle is so important for kids' growth. With practice, your students will eventually become accustomed to thinking more deeply on their own. You will see examples of other conversations like this one throughout this book as I illustrate how to teach the different strategies.

In the next chapter, we will examine the organization of the Reading Strategies Pyramid.

3

The Reading Strategies Pyramid

How It All Began

MANY YEARS AGO, WHILE I WAS SERVING AS A YOUTH leader in my church, I noticed the same problem that many of you experience today: my students had a lot of trouble understanding the Bible, so our discussions during lessons were unproductive and difficult. I was faced with a choice: one option was to water down my teaching so that I was doing all of the hard work, simply making my students receptacles of my biblical knowledge. With that option, however, I wondered how they would continue to grow in their relationship with God after they left my group if they were never being asked to do much beyond listening to me. So I chose another option: somehow, I needed to help these students comprehend the Bible for themselves. I had no idea how to do that, and none of the curriculum materials or youth ministry books I had were much help. In fact, it seemed like most of these resources were devoted to making Bible lessons more shallow and mostly entertaining for students, which was the exact opposite of what I was looking for!

So I prayed, "God, you know these kids better than anyone. How can I teach them so that they understand?" For the next 13 years, I continued to work with young people as a youth leader, Sunday School teacher, and elementary educator. God showed me how the reading strategies I was teaching at school could also help the youth at my church tackle the biblical text.

Even so, having a list of strategies to use didn't completely solve my problem. Which strategies were best? In what order should they be taught? How did the strategies relate to one another? Over many years, these questions led me to experiment, refine, and strengthen the method you see today: The Reading Strategies Pyramid.

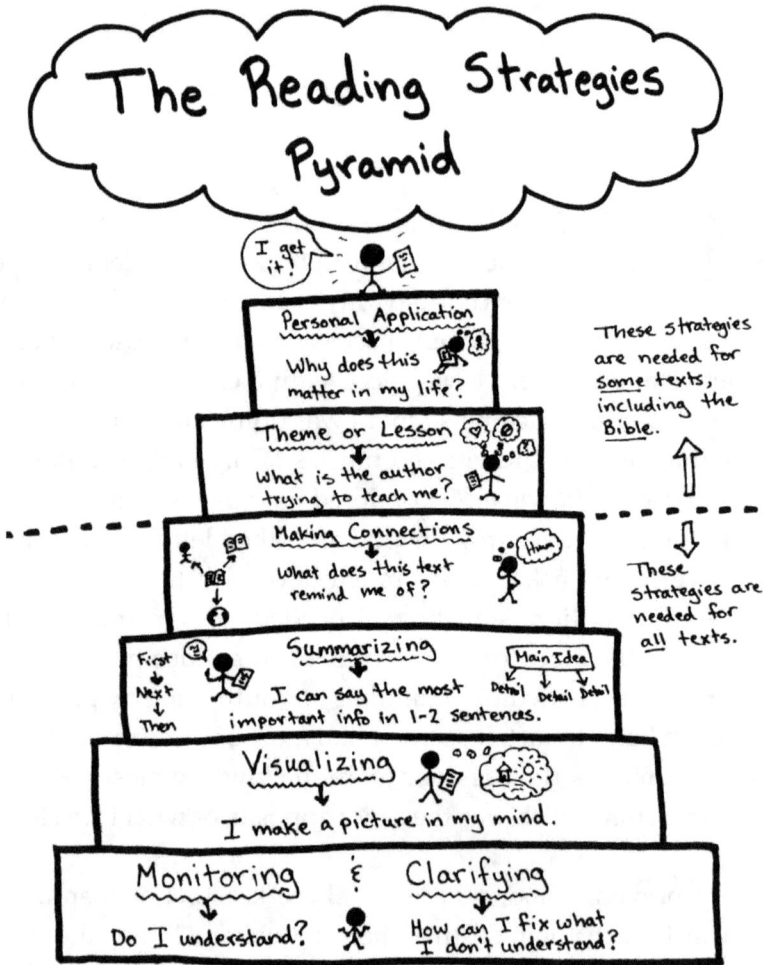

Visit www.biblicalliteracyforkids.com to download this graphic.

The Reading Strategies Pyramid is the main framework I created for teaching biblical literacy. It is my way of organizing those effective reading strategies in a way that is easy to use and simple to explain to kids. The rest of the book will focus on how to expertly guide students through each step of the pyramid.

You will notice that it is called the "Reading Strategies Pyramid," not the "*Biblical* Reading Strategies Pyramid." That is because this method can be used to develop a thorough comprehension of any type of text, not just the Bible. Most types of texts will not require readers to use every strategy listed. The Bible, however, is a more complex text and will require the use of every strategy. That is why a student who may devour fiction chapter books in her free time may still struggle with reading the Bible: a thorough understanding of the biblical text always requires the use of higher cognitive skills.

Organization of the Reading Strategies Pyramid

The Reading Strategies Pyramid is organized in a specific way. The skills are taught in order, purposefully moving from the bottom to the top. Monitoring and clarifying – often overlooked skills – form the base of the reader's understanding. Personal application is at the top because it depends on all of the strategies below it.

Recall the example from chapter one, when the Bible study leader was trying to get his group to answer the question, "How does this passage apply to our lives?" Examining the Reading Strategies Pyramid makes it easier to see why his group struggled so much. The group leader asked a few simple questions about the meaning of the text, which required group members to use basic monitoring, clarifying, and summarizing skills. But then he jumped to the top of the pyramid – personal application – without guiding the group through the skills of visualizing, making connections, and discovering the theme or lesson. One day, after much purposeful instruction, his group will be able to automatically move through these steps without much help. But at the beginning, participants will need to be intentionally guided through each step.

Troubleshooting: "Go Down to Go Up"

The Reading Strategies Pyramid can also provide leaders with a quick way to troubleshoot when students are struggling. For example, if a reader cannot summarize the passage, the leader should quickly jump down to visualizing (the skill right below summarizing) and ask the student to sketch what is happening in the text. If he is still stuck, the leader will know that the problem is really monitoring and clarifying – perhaps some of the words or phrases are causing confusion. Once the monitoring and clarifying problem has been fixed, the leader should be able to jump back up to the summarizing questions and continue the discussion from there.

This example illustrates my "Go Down to Go Up" rule: when students are stuck, I will go down a strategy (and keep going down if necessary) until I discover where they are confused. Once we resolve the problem, I can go back up to the strategy we are working on and continue to progress through the pyramid.

Modeling and Handing Off

At this point, you may be thinking, "These strategies sound great, but this also seems quite overwhelming for my students." Indeed, expecting readers to master all of these strategies *at once* is a recipe for disaster! This is when modeling and handing off become important tools for avoiding student overwhelm.

Modeling is when adults demonstrate how to do the strategy using writing, pictures, and thinking aloud. Since your readers are still developing so many cognitive skills, you can support them by narrating what you are thinking as you use a specific strategy. Hearing how an adult is thinking gives readers a glimpse into more mature thought processes so that students can imitate them.

For example, let's imagine that a group of readers is tackling Genesis 3, the Fall of Man. If the adult is modeling the visualizing strategy, which involves drawing what is happening in the passage, he might say, "I notice that the characters in this story are Adam,

Eve, the snake, and God. So I'm going to draw them. The tree and the garden are part of the setting, so I will also add those to my sketch." This helps students understand how the adult chose which elements to add to his drawing and which to leave out.

Narrating thinking is also helpful for more complex skills, or when the adult's conclusion is less obvious. For instance, modeling making connections for Genesis 3 might sound like this:

"In verse 15, God tells the snake, 'I will put enmity between you and the woman, and between your offspring and hers; he will crush your head, and you will strike his heel.' We know that the snake is Satan, so God is saying that a child of the woman will crush his head or somehow destroy him. But Satan will 'strike his heel,' or somehow hurt the child. This reminds me of what happened when Jesus was on the cross: Jesus was a woman's offspring, and he defeated Satan. But Satan also hurt Jesus through all of the suffering He experienced on the cross."

Notice that the adult is doing all of the hard work during modeling. This is good for students at first so they can understand what they are supposed to be doing when they are using the strategy. The example in the previous paragraph is a good demonstration of this since most students will never make the connection between Genesis and the Gospels without modeling from an adult. This type of thinking aloud shows students what to look for. However, if the adults continuously do all of the hard work and only model, the readers will not grow in biblical literacy. This is where handing off comes in.

Handing off is a method that helps readers practice their new skills well. **Handing off is the process the adult uses to gradually turn over "thinking responsibility" to the students.** For any skill, the adult will first *model* the thinking and strategies. Later, the adult will invite the readers to do the strategy with her through discussion and other shared tasks. Finally, after sufficient practice together, students will be expected to complete the strategy on their own. Let's look at an example of how this process may look over time.

At first...

Student Responsibility	Students and Adults Together	Adult Modeling
	• Monitoring & Clarifying • Visualizing	• Summarizing • Making Connections • Theme/Lesson • Personal Application

After some practice...

Student Responsibility	Students and Adults Together	Adult Modeling
• Monitoring & Clarifying • Visualizing	• Summarizing	• Making Connections • Theme/Lesson • Personal Application

Later...

Student Responsibility	Students and Adults Together	Adult Modeling
• Monitoring & Clarifying • Visualizing • Summarizing	• Making Connections	• Theme/Lesson • Personal Application

Notice that readers will grow in their responsibilities, taking on more and more strategies on their own. You and the students will only work together on one or two strategies at a time. Exploring the focus strategy or strategies will be the bulk of your lesson with them. Eventually, you will arrive at a point where your lessons look more like this:

Student Responsibility	Students and Adults Together	Adult Modeling
• Monitoring & Clarifying • Visualizing • Summarizing • Making Connections	• Theme/Lesson • Personal Application	

At this point, you won't need to model strategies, and your conversations with students will be much more in depth. You will be able to ask questions about any strategy, such as, "What connections did you make?" or "How do you know that's the theme?" or "How does this passage influence your life?" Your readers' blank stares of confusion will be a thing of the past! And if they get stuck, they will have the tools they need to get unstuck. Students at this stage, if they are old enough, will also be ready to tackle hard questions and more obscure passages of the Bible. It is a beautiful time when the "How to Read the Bible" instruction ends and the focus becomes solely on the meaning of the text. This is when your students' spiritual growth will truly accelerate.

In the next chapter, we'll look more closely at the strategies at the base of the Reading Strategies Pyramid: monitoring and clarifying.

4

Monitoring and Clarifying

ONITORING AND CLARIFYING ARE FOUND AT THE BOT-
tom of the Reading Strategies Pyramid because they are
foundational to reading comprehension. **Monitoring is when the reader pays attention to whether or not he understands the text.** If the reader determines that something is confusing, he needs to use a clarifying strategy. **Clarifying is when the reader uses a tool to clear up her confusion about the text,** such as consulting a dictionary, Bible handbook, an adult, or other tools. Together, monitoring and clarifying form a gateway to understanding all types of texts; without them, students are simply letting the words pass before their eyes without thought.

Young readers and struggling readers are less likely to use monitoring and clarifying strategies without prompting because they are overly concerned with trying to just read the words. Older students can sometimes be resistant to using monitoring and clarifying strategies because they don't want to appear "stupid." Others just don't want to be bothered with using a strategy and are content to understand less of the text. Therefore, it is imperative that adults normalize the use of tools in reading through modeling and practice. For example, if you and the students have been repeatedly practicing how to use a dictionary, they are more likely to use one on their own without negative feelings.

Sometimes spotting readers who are struggling with monitoring and clarifying can be tough unless you ask them about specific words and phrases. One potential reason is that many readers are familiar with all of the words in the passage, so they equate familiarity with comprehension without truly understanding the meanings of the words. For instance, consider this example from Psalm 1:1-3:

> Blessed is the one
> who does not walk in step with the wicked
> or stand in the way that sinners take
> or sit in the company of mockers,
> but whose delight is in the law of the Lord,
> and who meditates on his law day and night.
> That person is like a tree planted by streams of water,
> which yields its fruit in season
> and whose leaf does not wither—
> whatever they do prospers.

Example Conversation:

Adult: Did you understand that passage?

Student: Yep.

Adult: Let's look more closely at some of the words here. Have you heard the word "mocker" before?

Student: Yes.

Adult: Great! What does it mean?

Student: I don't know.

Adult: What about "yields"? What does that mean?

Student: I'm not sure.

Adult: Okay, let's see if we can use some tools to help us...

This type of conversation invites students to take a second look at familiar words to determine if they really understand what's being said. Adults should be aware that many of the religious words that fill our church services and the pages of the Bible are actually not well understood by readers. Here are some of the most common confusing words I have encountered while teaching students:

Common Religious Words that Confuse Students	
• Blessed	• Praise
• Covenant	• Priest
• Doxology	• Prophet, prophecy
• Faith, faithful, faithfulness	• Psalm
• Favor	• Reconcile, reconciliation
• Fool, folly	• Repent, repentance
• Glory, glorify	• Righteous, righteousness
• Grace	• Sabbath
• Holy, holiness	• Sacrifice
• Idolatry	• Sanctification
• Immoral, immorality	• Saved, salvation
• Incarnation	• Sin, sinful
• Iniquity	• Sovereign
• Judgment	• Tabernacle, temple
• Justification	• Tempt, temptation
• Offering	• Wisdom
• Persecute, persecution	• Woe

The above list is not exhaustive; it is designed to help you think about how many everyday religious words can be hard for your readers. Notice that the word "saved" is often a confusing word – and this is true even for kids who have been a part of the church their whole lives! I have found that when I ask students to explain what it means to be "saved," they will usually say something like, "Go to heaven when I die." If I really press them for details on *how* a person is saved (which, in the Christian context, is central to the meaning of the word), they will often uncomfortably reply, "I don't know." Rarely do students mention that being "saved" means that you have a growing relationship with God, both in this life and in the life to come. This is just one example of how stopping to unpack familiar religious words can lead to extremely important instruction, as well as how detrimental it is to skip over teaching vocabulary just because students appear to understand.

Text Complexity

As we have just discussed, making sure your readers actually understand the words in the text is very important. But sometimes the version of the Bible a student is reading is unnecessarily difficult, preventing the reader from understanding the majority of the important words in a passage. This can get frustrating and tedious very quickly for both the student and the adult. Of course, the adult can stop and explain every word, but a better way to reduce some of the difficulty is to address the issue of text complexity.

Text complexity refers to the difficulty of the reading material, both in its vocabulary and subject matter. Even though monitoring and clarifying are incredibly important strategies, students shouldn't be forced to rely on them too frequently while reading. Have you ever had to read something where you had to keep looking up words, or where the words made sense but the concept was beyond you? It's quite aggravating! Students can have this experience even more frequently than adults. To build biblical literacy, students need to be appropriately matched to a Bible at their *reading level*, not necessarily at their age level. This keeps reading from becoming frustrating. Otherwise, the high text complexity will get in the way of understanding the meaning and encourage reading avoidance.

It is far better for young readers to tackle a children's Bible translation now with less aggravation than to struggle through a more common "adult" version. They can always move up to a harder, more literal Bible translation as their skills progress. After all, this process already requires them to grow in complex *thinking* skills, so it is unproductive to use a version with words that are so difficult that they get in the way of comprehension.

Whatever version you choose to use, make sure to research not only the translation's accuracy but also the reading level of the text. Two common children's Bible versions are the New International Reader's Version (NIrV) and the International Children's Bible (ICB). The NIrV and the ICB have both been translated to a third-grade reading level. In contrast, the very popular New International Version (NIV) is translated at a seventh-grade reading level, and the King James Version has been translated to a twelfth-grade reading level.[1] When in doubt, opt for a lower level to help your students learn the biblical literacy strategies more easily.

Confusion on Three Levels

In my experience, three main types of confusion pop up when reading a text. The first, and most simple to deal with, is that the student cannot read, or decode, a word. This is called **decoding-dependent confusion**. Simply helping the reader sound out the word quickly resolves this kind of confusion. As we just discussed in the previous section, much decoding-dependent confusion can be avoided by matching students to a Bible with appropriate text complexity. Even with a Bible on their reading level, students may still need help with names and technical terms.

The second type of confusion students can experience is when they can read a word but do not know its meaning. This is **vocabulary-dependent confusion**. These confusing words might be some of those religious words discussed earlier, or they may be everyday words that the student has not yet learned. Vocabulary-dependent confusion can be easily resolved by using a dictionary or asking an adult for the word's meaning.

The third and most complex problem for students is when they understand all of the individual word meanings, but together the words in the text still do not make sense. This is **background-knowledge-dependent confusion**. In this type of confusion, readers do not have enough background knowledge (sometimes called prior knowledge) to access the text's meaning. Sometimes this is a lack of knowledge about Bible times, and sometimes it is just a lack of the life experience needed to grasp the concept. One common place to encounter this type of confusion is when reading the book of Leviticus. Readers must have a thorough understanding of the entire book of Exodus, in addition to a knowledge of the customs of that time, or the text will be incomprehensible.

But the need for background knowledge is not limited to difficult Old Testament books. Consider this example from Matthew 9:9-13:

> As Jesus went on from there, he saw a man named Matthew sitting at the tax collector's booth. "Follow me," he told him, and Matthew got up and followed him.
>
> While Jesus was having dinner at Matthew's house, many tax collectors and sinners came and ate with him and his disciples. When the Pharisees saw this, they asked his disciples, "Why does your teacher eat with tax collectors and sinners?"
>
> On hearing this, Jesus said, "It is not the healthy who need a doctor, but the sick. But go and learn what this means: 'I desire mercy, not sacrifice.' For I have not come to call the righteous, but sinners."

Here, depending on their ages, students may encounter some decoding-dependent confusion with the word "Pharisees." They may also have some vocabulary-dependent confusion and need help with words such as "tax collector" or "mercy." But most of the confusion is likely to be background-knowledge-dependent. Questions you should ask students include:

- Why is it a big deal that Matthew is a tax collector?
- Why do the Pharisees care who Jesus is eating with?
- Why is Jesus talking about healthy and sick people?
- What sacrifices is Jesus talking about?

- Why does Jesus say he doesn't want righteous people?

These types of questions model how readers should think about the passage. Most students will not even realize that they didn't understand what they needed to, or that some words like "healthy" and "sick" have deeper meanings here. It's so easy for them to let those words just pass before their eyes without thought! So you are coaching them to pay attention to the details they don't know. With practice, readers will become better at noticing when they need more background knowledge and asking for clarification.

For background-knowledge-dependent confusion, students can use study Bibles, Bible handbooks, or ask an adult for help. As they read more of the Bible and become familiar with God's larger story, they will have less trouble with background knowledge.

I've created a chart that easily lays out the different types of confusion, how to spot them, and how to address them.

Type of Confusion	How It Sounds in a Lesson	Tools and Resources
Decoding-Dependent	• "What does this word say?" • Misreading words	• Adult helps in sounding out words correctly
Vocabulary-Dependent	• "What does this word mean?" • Unable to explain the meaning of the word when asked (like those religious words)	• Dictionary • Adult
Background-Knowledge-Dependent	• "I don't get this whole passage!"	• Bible handbooks • Study Bible notes • Pictures

	Inability to answer questions even after figuring out confusing words.	Diagrams • Timelines • Adult

Marking Up the Page

When students are just beginning to learn monitoring and clarifying strategies, it is very helpful for them to be able to mark up the text. Therefore, I advise you to print a copy of the short section of text you are working on for each reader. As they read, students should:

1. Circle confusing words. These can be words they can't read or words they don't understand. (Decoding-dependent and vocabulary-dependent confusion)

2. Put a star next to longer sections that are confusing. (Background-knowledge-dependent confusion)

As students use the suggested resources and tools to clear up their confusion, they can add their clarifying notes right on the page. Check out the lesson examples at the end of this chapter to see what a student's work might look like.

Of course, you don't want to be printing Bible passages forever; otherwise, students can become dependent on you providing the pages and feel intimidated when they are reading passages they can't write on. So as soon as your readers become comfortable using monitoring and clarifying strategies, they can begin to use a piece of paper to take notes about whatever is confusing. You will know that your students are ready for you to stop printing passages when they no longer need to mark up so many words during your discussions. Let's look at an example from my class of a student taking notes on a regular piece of paper.

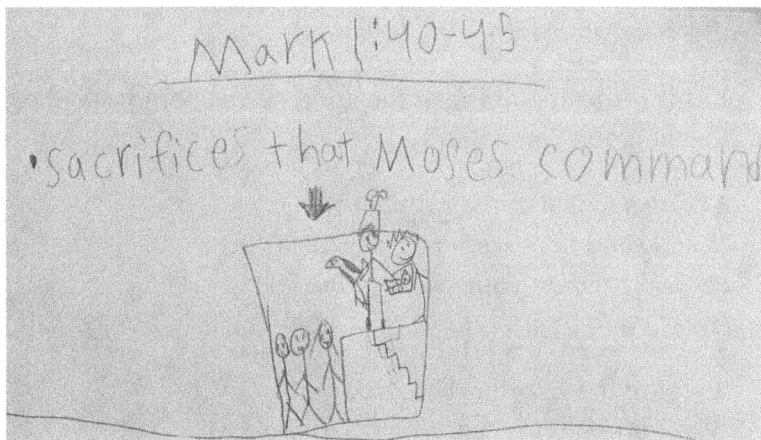

This student was confused about the "sacrifices that Moses commanded" mentioned in the passage she was reading. Instead of writing on the text, she wrote the phrase down and then drew a picture of the sacrifices as she learned more about them.

Once your students reach the higher levels of the Reading Strategies Pyramid, they may not even need to take notes about what is confusing. Ideally, they will just notice what's confusing and seek clarification.

Lesson Examples

Let's take a look at some lesson examples from a third-grade student who is brand new to the monitoring and clarifying strategies. These examples can give you an idea of what your first lessons with students might be like. At the end of the example conversations, you will see a picture of the student's work on this text.

The adult had originally planned for this passage, Mark 1:1-8, to be taught in one lesson. However, using the strategies took much longer than she had anticipated, so she broke up the discussion into two different sessions. This is important. Don't be afraid to break up a passage if your readers need it. Your students' attention spans can only handle so much at once!

Lesson Passage: Mark 1:1-8 (NIrV):

1 This is the beginning of the good news about Jesus the Messiah, the Son of God.

2 Long ago Isaiah the prophet wrote,
"I will send my messenger ahead of you.
He will prepare your way." (Mal. 3:1)

3 "A messenger is calling out in the desert,
'Prepare the way for the Lord.
Make straight paths for him.'" (Isa. 40:3)

4 And so John the Baptist appeared in the desert. He preached that people should be baptized and turn away from their sins. Then God would forgive them. **5** All the people from the countryside of Judea went out to him. All the people from Jerusalem went too. When they admitted they had sinned, John baptized them in the Jordan River. **6** John wore clothes made out of camel's hair. He had a leather belt around his waist. And he ate locusts and wild honey. **7** Here is what John was preaching. "After me, there is someone coming who is more powerful than I am. I'm not good enough to bend down and untie his sandals. **8** I baptize you with water. But he will baptize you with the Holy Spirit."

Lesson Teaching and Discussion: Session One

First, the student read the passage aloud. She was prompted to circle confusing words and star confusing sentences and phrases. As expected, since this was her first time using these strategies, she marked nothing on her own. Here is the discussion that followed:

Adult: Did you find anything confusing?

Student: Nope!

Adult: Great! What's happening in the passage?

Student: Uh…I don't know.

Adult: Okay, let's look more closely at the passage. Can you read verses 1-2 again?

[Student reads]

Adult: What's a prophet?

Student: Someone who speaks for God.

Adult: Good! And who is the prophet here?

Student: Isaiah.

Adult: Yes! What did he write?

Student: I don't know.

Adult: *[Pointing at verses 2b-3]* See how this is indented with quotation marks? Mark, who wrote this book, is using those to show you that these are the sentences that Isaiah wrote. Can you read them again?

[Student reads verses 2b-3]

Adult: Great! Now, see how the first word that Isaiah wrote is "I"? It says, "I will send my messenger…" But who is "I"?

Student: I don't know.

Adult: Well, Isaiah is a prophet, right? What does a prophet do again?

Student: A prophet speaks for God. Oh! Then "I" would be…God?

Adult: Yes! Very good! Circle "I" and write "God" above it. Now it says that God is sending a messenger – do we know who that is?

Student: No.

Adult: Maybe if we read closely, we will figure it out. Now it says that the messenger will go ahead of "you." Who is "you"?

Student: Maybe Isaiah?

Adult: Maybe. Let's keep reading closely and see if the passage will tell us. What does it say that the messenger will do?

Student: *[Reading]* Prepare your way…be in the desert…make straight paths…

Adult: Stop! Do you know what "make straight paths" means?

Student: No.

Adult: Put a star next to that phrase because it is confusing. "Make straight paths" means that the messenger is making it easy for this person to come, just like how it's easier for you to walk on a straight path than a crooked one. *[The adult and student discuss several examples of paths that they know.]* Now, write "make it easy for him to come" above "make straight paths."

[Student writes]

Adult: Okay, now verse three says, "Prepare the way for the…?"

Student: The Lord!

Adult: Good! So go back to the beginning of Isaiah's writing. It says, "I will send my messenger ahead of you. He will prepare your way." Now do we know who the "you" is?

Student: The Lord!

Adult: Great! Circle "you" and write "Lord" above it.

[Student writes]

Adult: Now, let's see what we've discovered. *[The adult paraphrases using the student's notes.]* Isaiah the prophet wrote that God will send his messenger ahead of the Lord. The messenger will prepare the Lord's way. A messenger is calling out in the desert, "Prepare the way for the Lord! Make it easy for him to come!" Now, I wonder who this messenger is and why they're in the desert? I guess we'll find out next time...

Whew! That was a lot of work to understand just a few verses! Notice that the adult is doing quite a bit of questioning that forces the student to look back at the text. This is very intentional. The adult is teaching the student that the Bible is *rich with detail,* so she must slow down to understand it well. The adult will not always have to do so much prompting and questioning, but it is necessary in the beginning.

The student is using a resource to understand what she doesn't know – the adult's brain! Eventually, the adult will teach the student how to use more resources. At first, though, it's more important for the student to focus on noticing what she doesn't know.

The adult decided to go over this passage in two different sessions because she could tell that this young student's brain was getting tired and distracted. Keeping students engaged, but not overwhelmed, is an important part of the teaching process. The student will be able to tolerate longer sessions and passages as her skills grow.

Now, let's find out how the second session with this passage went.

Lesson Teaching and Discussion: Session Two

[The adult and student reread Mark 1:1-8 and review what they discussed last time.]

> **Adult:** So we were trying to figure out who the messenger is, right? Where was the messenger supposed to be?
>
> **Student**: *[Looking back at verses 2-3]* In the desert.
>
> **Adult:** Right! Let's keep reading to see if we can figure out who the messenger is.
>
> **Student**: *[Reading verse 4]* "And so John the Baptist appeared in the desert..." Oh! I think the messenger is John the Baptist!
>
> **Adult:** Why?
>
> **Student:** Because he's in the desert!
>
> **Adult:** Interesting. What else was the messenger supposed to do besides hang out in the desert?
>
> **Student:** *[Reading her notes]* Make it easy for the Lord to come.
>
> **Adult:** Let's keep reading to see if John does that.
>
> **Student:** *[After reading verses 4-8]* He does!
>
> **Adult:** How does he do that?

Student: He baptizes people and tells them about God.

Adult: Would that make it easier for the Lord to come?

Student: Yes.

The adult and student then have a discussion about who "the Lord" is. The student knows it's God, but she doesn't comprehend that the text means "Jesus." She also doesn't understand what "baptize you with the Holy Spirit" means. She just doesn't have enough background knowledge yet to figure these things out. The adult decides not to explain these concepts and tells the student that she will discover more as she continues to read Mark in the next few sessions.

> **Adult:** Now we know who the messenger is! Circle "messenger" in verse three and write "John the Baptist" above it.

> *[Student writes]*

> *[Student and adult reread the passage]*

> **Adult:** So Mark is telling us that Isaiah wrote about what John the Baptist would say and do, and then it actually happened! That's amazing since Isaiah wrote this hundreds of years before John the Baptist was alive! This shows me that God really does know everything that's going to happen. It can help me trust Him because He is in control.

the prophet wrote,

God   Lord

"I will send my messenger ahead of you.

    He will prepare your way." (Malachi 3:1)

~John the Baptist
3 "A messenger is calling out in the desert,

'Prepare the way for the Lord.
    make it easy for him to come
    Make straight paths for him.'" (Isaiah 40:3)

4 And so John the Baptist appeared in the desert. He preached that pe

turn away from their sins. Then God would forgive them. 5 All the peop

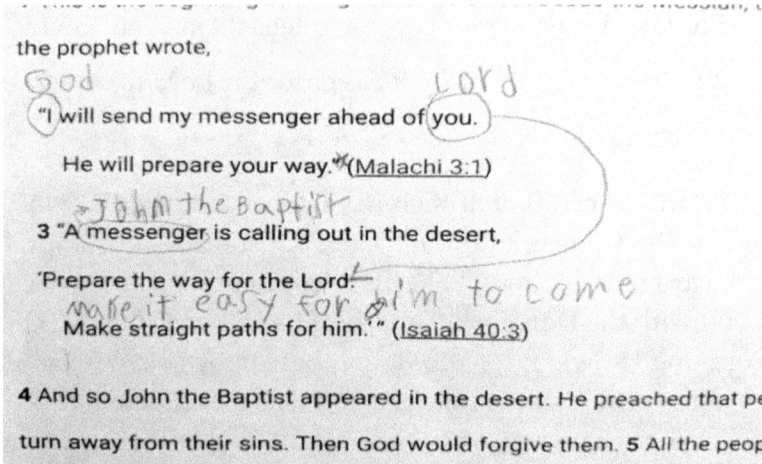

The student's work after finishing both lessons. You can see how she is writing her notes directly on her copy of the passage.

Notice that the adult continues to call the student's attention to the details of the text and prompts her to use monitoring and clarifying strategies. At the end, the adult *summarizes* what the passage was about and provides a *personal application*. The student is not expected to use these strategies yet but simply to listen to the adult model them.

Remember, these lesson examples are from the student's first experience with monitoring and clarifying strategies. Because of this, the adult relied more on conversation, rather than tools like handbooks or dictionaries, to clear up confusion. As the reader improves, more tools will be added. Students will *not* always need this much support. You will know when your students have mastered these strategies when they notice their own confusion without prompting and take the necessary steps to fix it.

Strategy Best Friends

Monitoring and clarifying are great strategies, but if that's all you do with students in every session, it can leave them feeling like they didn't accomplish much. For this reason, I always teach the strategies of monitoring, clarifying, and visualizing together. Incorporating the visualizing strategies at the same time gives students a pictorial record of the discussion; it is a tangible reminder that they actually learned something. It also helps cement the passage's meaning into their minds. In the next chapter, we will closely examine the visualizing strategy and discover its importance in the Reading Strategies Pyramid.

---

[1] Christianbook. "Translation Reading Levels." Accessed June 20, 2025. https://www.christianbook.com/page/bibles/about-bibles/bible-translation-reading-levels.

5

Visualizing

THE SECOND STEP UP ON THE READING STRATEGIES PYR-
amid is visualizing. **Visualizing is when the reader makes a
picture in his mind of what is happening in the text.** This is
different from summarizing, which we will get to in the next chapter, because visualizing simply asks students to picture events or
concepts from the text. Visualizing does not require students to
identify what is most important.

Strong readers create a "mental movie" of the passage as they
read it. For a narrative text, visualizing helps them "see" the characters and action in the story. Much of the Old Testament and the Gospels fall into the category of narrative nonfiction – a retelling of true
events in a story format. Two other broad genres are expository (informational) and persuasive texts. For these, visualizing helps students picture complex topics and ideas. Many of the New Testament
letters to the churches fall into these categories. Of course, there are
many genres in the Bible, but the purpose of this strategy remains
the same: make an image in your mind of what you are reading.

Readers who do not visualize are likely to become frustrated
with more lengthy texts. To them, these longer passages are just a
confusing jumble of words. Younger readers who are transitioning
from picture books to chapter books commonly encounter this difficulty. That's because in picture books, the illustrator does the visualizing for the student. But when transitioning to chapter books and
other longer texts, the student is suddenly expected to visualize on
her own. For this reason, a long, pictureless text can seem particularly daunting to young or struggling readers.

However, supporting readers in visualizing is not difficult: after reading a short section of the text, ask the students to make a quick sketch about what they have read. Some students may do one drawing, while others may do a few comic book-style drawings. (You may need to set a timer for some students so they don't take all day creating their "art project.") Once students have finished, ask them to explain their drawings to you. Take note of what they understood well and what they missed. Redirect them back to the text to pick up any important details they have forgotten.

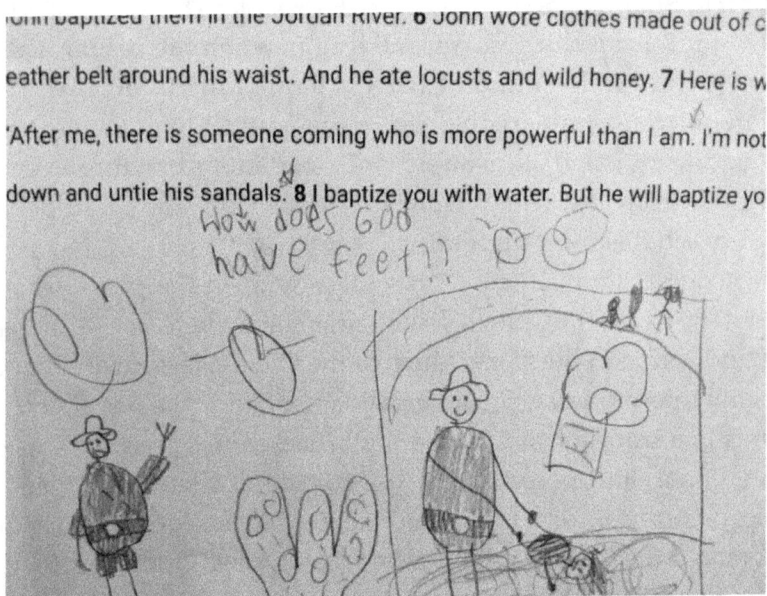

The student's picture after discussion of the Mark 1:1-8 passage about John the Baptist from the last chapter. Her drawings show that she has picked up many of the important details from the passage. She is still confused about how God can have feet because she hasn't yet figured out that "the Lord" in the passage is Jesus.

Remember, visualizing is a skill because it forces students to actually think about what they've read and synthesize it into another form – from words to pictures. While many readers will pick up on this strategy with little guidance, some learners, such as those with attention difficulties or special needs, may require more support to pick up on all of the important details. For these, more time with repeated practicing and modeling from you may be all that is needed for success.

Adults can model visualizing in two ways, using the *think-aloud method* or the *collaborative method*. Let's use the Mark 1:1-8 passage about John the Baptist from chapter four to examine these two methods.

If the adult chooses to use the think-aloud method, she will narrate what she notices and draw a picture for the students. Then the students will copy her picture. This can be particularly appropriate when students are first learning to visualize and aren't sure what they should include in their pictures.

Using this method might sound something like this: "When I read this passage, I noticed that John was preaching and baptizing people, so I'm going to include both of those actions in my drawing. The passage also said that he wore clothes made of camel's hair and a leather belt. So I will make sure to draw him that way." After narrating her thinking, the adult will create a simple drawing and have the students copy it. Remember, fantastic art skills are not necessary. Stick figures are great!

The adult can also choose the collaborative method to model visualizing. This method entails just what it sounds like: the adult and student read the passage and work together to decide what should be included in their drawing. This can be a good next step after students have had some experience with visualizing. It might sound something like this:

> **Adult:** What important things is John the Baptist doing in this passage?
>
> **Student:** He's preaching and baptizing people.
>
> **Adult:** Right. We need to include both of those in our drawing. How should we do that? Should we try to make one big drawing or more than one drawing, like a comic book?

Student: Well, since he's doing more than one thing, we should probably have more than one drawing.

Adult: Good idea. How should we draw John the Baptist? Were there any clues in the passage about what he looks like?

Student: He has weird clothes.

Adult: Yes! Like what?

Student: He has camel hair clothes and a leather belt.

Adult: Great! Let's make sure we draw him that way.

Then the student and adult will create their drawings together.

It is important to remember that visualizing is the second step, and not the foundation, of the Reading Strategies Pyramid. If a student is struggling to visualize, especially if he typically doesn't have trouble with this strategy, go down one step on the Pyramid: he is likely having a problem with monitoring and clarifying, which is preventing solid comprehension. Difficult words, phrases, or the lack of background knowledge must be addressed *before* a reader can correctly visualize. Use the methods outlined in chapter four to clear up confusion before moving on.

Mark 1:9-13

Jesus Is Baptized and Tempted

9 At that time Jesus came from Nazareth in Galilee. John baptized Jesus in the Jordan River. 10 Jesus was coming up out of the water. Just then he saw heaven being torn open. Jesus saw the H Spirit coming down on him like a dove. 11 A voice spoke to him from heaven. It said, "You are my S and I love you. I am very pleased with you."

12 At once the Holy Spirit sent Jesus out into the desert. 13 He was in the desert 40 days. There Satan tempted him. The wild animals didn't harm Jesus. Angels took care of him.

↳ Read Luke 4:1-13
together. :)

An example of a student's visualizing of a passage. She wanted to know more about how Jesus was tempted, so we read some of Luke 4 together as noted on the page. She included those details in her drawing.

Once students become skilled at visualizing, making them sketch out their pictures is not necessary. If you are confident that students are using the strategy mentally, then sharing sketches can be reserved for more cumbersome passages.

Now we will examine another important step in the Reading Strategies Pyramid: summarizing.

6

Summarizing

THE THIRD STEP UP ON THE READING STRATEGIES PYRA-mid is summarizing. This is an essential skill not only in read-ing but for all of life. **Summarizing is when the reader can tell you the most important things about a passage in just a few sentences.**

The writer in me cringes at using the very nonspecific word "things" in that definition, but the usage of that word is actually pur-poseful. This is because the "things" a reader is looking for change with the genre of the text. For example, in narrative text, the student will be looking for the most important *events* from the story and ex-plaining them in proper sequence. In expository (informational) or persuasive texts, the reader is looking for the *main idea* and the most important *details* that support the main idea. Therefore, knowing the genre of the text is quite helpful for students because they will know what they are looking for: events or main idea and details. Use of a study Bible or Bible Handbook can be very helpful in determining the genre because many include that information in their introduc-tion of each biblical book.

But just knowing the genre of a passage will not automatically turn students into excellent summarizers. They will also need to un-derstand the difference between *summarizing* and *retelling*. Perhaps you have had the opportunity to ask a talkative young girl about her day. She will gladly tell you every single detail: "First I woke up, then I played. Then I ate oatmeal. Then I brushed my teeth. Then I..." Ten minutes later, you may have only arrived at the specifics of lunchtime! *This child is retelling.* She is explaining every single thing that happened without regard to the importance of the details.

Every child starts here, but they cannot stay in the "Land of Retelling" forever. Life is far too complex for simple retelling, and students will quickly become overwhelmed by all of the details if this is the only skill they know. The ability to summarize is crucial because it synthesizes information into bite-sized chunks that the reader can remember. While some kids will develop this skill without much guidance, most have to be directly taught how to differentiate between essential and nonessential information. This becomes easier as students develop more abstract thinking skills, typically around eight or nine years old.

Purposeful instruction is vital to help students master the skill of summarizing. Here are the steps to use with students when they are first learning this strategy:

1. Choose a short narrative text to practice with first because narratives are easiest to summarize. (Later, you will introduce other genres.)

2. Before you begin teaching this passage to students, write your own short summary of the passage. You need to know exactly what the summary should be so that you can guide students to discover it.

3. Read the passage with the students, using monitoring and clarifying strategies as needed.

4. Ask students to visualize by drawing what they have read.

5. Explain what summarizing is, using the definition I provided at the beginning of the chapter or by putting it into your own words. Ask, "What are the most important *events* in this passage?"

6. Lead your students in a discussion of the important events. If students can't decide which events are important, ask, "If ____ (event) wasn't in the story,

would the story still make sense?" You can also point out which events the students included in their drawing from the visualizing step. If they still cannot determine what is most important, model for them by saying, "I know that _____ is important because..." or "I know that _____ is not important because..."

7. Verbally summarize with the students. Use the summary you created beforehand as a guide, but be flexible with the wording – if students noticed an important detail or explained something in a slightly different way, substitute their words for yours. Write the summary down and have the students copy it.

Let's look at an example of this process using Mark 3:1-6 (NIrV):

Another time Jesus went into the synagogue. A man with a weak and twisted hand was there. Some Pharisees were trying to find fault with Jesus. They watched him closely. They wanted to see if he would heal the man on the Sabbath day. Jesus spoke to the man with the weak and twisted hand. "Stand up in front of everyone," he said.

Then Jesus asked them, "What does the Law say we should do on the Sabbath day? Should we do good? Or should we do evil? Should we save life? Or should we kill?" But no one answered.

Jesus looked around at them in anger. He was very upset because their hearts were stubborn. Then he said to the man, "Stretch out your hand." He stretched it out, and his hand had become as good as new. Then the Pharisees went out and began to make plans with the Herodians. They wanted to kill Jesus.

Why did I choose this passage? When I am working with young students, the first book we study is Mark since it is a narrative text and the retelling of Jesus' life is more simple than the other Gospels. By the time we get to the third chapter, my readers should definitely be ready for summarizing if they have not started learning this skill already.

After choosing the passage, I need to figure out what an appropriate, student-friendly summary will be. My summary is:

> Jesus heals a man with a twisted hand on the Sabbath day. Now the Pharisees want to kill him.

I write this summary in my lesson notes before I meet with my students.

Next, I read this passage with my students during our lesson time. We use monitoring and clarifying strategies to make sure we understand everything in the text. I make sure to discuss the words "Herodians," "Pharisees," and "Sabbath," along with the phrase "trying to find fault." Students use the visualizing strategy to draw pictures of what is happening in the story.

Then I ask the students to tell me the important events in the story. One eager – and talkative – student raises her hand and answers, "In this story, Jesus goes to the synagogue place and there's this guy there with a messed-up hand. And the Pharisees want to find Jesus doing something wrong, so they're watching him. And then Jesus brings the guy up and starts asking if we should do good or evil on the Sabbath, and he gets mad because of the Pharisees. So then he heals the man, and now the Pharisees and Herodians want to kill him."

Clearly, monitoring, clarifying, and visualizing have done their magic: the student understands the passage. But the problem is that she is retelling; in fact, her "summary" is nearly as long as the passage itself! So I remind my students what summarizing is. We read the definition from the Reading Strategies Pyramid. I say, "Pretend you have to explain this story to a group of kindergarteners. You know that they can only pay attention to a few sentences at a time.

What are the most important things the kindergarteners would need to know?"

Then we reread the passage and make a list of the most important events. Here is our list:

Important Events

- Jesus goes to the synagogue.
- The Pharisees want to find something wrong with Jesus.
- Jesus heals a man with a twisted hand.
- Now the Pharisees and the Herodians are planning to kill Jesus.

Now, we use our important events list to create a summary. We discuss how some of the wording of our summary could go. I take their ideas into account. I noticed that they are focused on the fact that the Pharisees want to find something wrong with Jesus, probably because we discussed the phrase "trying to find fault" when we were reading the passage. So I make sure to add that detail into our summary, even though it was not in my original one. The summary we created together is:

> The Pharisees want to find something wrong with Jesus. Jesus heals a man with a twisted hand on the Sabbath even though the Pharisees think that's wrong. Now they want to kill him.

This summary is longer than my original, but capturing the students' ideas is very important; it shows them that they are the ones who are really doing the work of comprehending the text. This new summary still meets the requirements of only being a few sentences long. For the last step, all students write down the summary we created together on the same paper with their visualizing pictures.

With practice, students will become adept at writing their own summaries and will no longer need to do that step together with you. Also, they may not always need to visualize on paper (because they are doing it mentally), allowing them to move on to the summarizing step more quickly. When students reach that point, you can begin to read much longer passages of text with students. You will still need to break it up, stopping every so often to ask, "Who can summarize this section?" But because students at that stage will not be bogged down by drawing everything they read, you can get through many summaries in one sitting, which allows readers to have a broader understanding of longer passages of the Bible.

Why Write It Down?

The most common question about teaching summarizing is: Why write out the summaries? Isn't verbally summarizing enough? When students are first learning to summarize, writing down their summaries is essential for several reasons. First, it forces students to create coherent thoughts. After all, some people's verbal summaries can be quite rambling! A written summary also allows you to check the reader's comprehension quickly and easily.

Second, the written summary will help students retain the information they learned from the passage because they will have a record to refer back to later on. During their next session, when you ask, "What happened in the last passage we read?" you will no longer have to suffer the blank stares of confusion. They can simply review their summaries! Written summaries are also particularly useful when students are learning to make connections, which we will discuss in the next chapter.

This young student includes a very simple summary next to her visualization.

Given the benefits of written summaries, you may decide to always have students write a short summary as part of a Bible Journal. However, remember that writing is *not* the ultimate goal: understanding is. Writing is simply a tool to aid comprehension.

Now let's focus on the fourth step in the Reading Strategies Pyramid: making connections.

7

Making Connections

THE FOURTH STEP UP ON THE READING STRATEGIES PYRamid is making connections. This step marks an exciting transition in your reader's progress in comprehension. The first three steps – monitoring and clarifying, visualizing, and summarizing – are all about getting students to digest and then regurgitate exactly what the author has written. But the top steps of the Pyramid – making connections, theme or lesson, and personal application – are all about the reader thinking deeply about the text and using its content in his or her daily life. Making connections is the first step toward this more complex way of thinking about reading.

Making connections is when the reader explains how the text reminds him of something else that he knows about. At first glance, this may seem like an insignificant skill. In reality, making connections is an extremely powerful tool that allows students to begin to understand the relevance of what they are reading.

There are three types of connections: *text-to-self, text-to-text, and text-to-world*. Each type makes a unique contribution to the reader's comprehension. Let's examine each type in turn and discover its importance to biblical literacy.

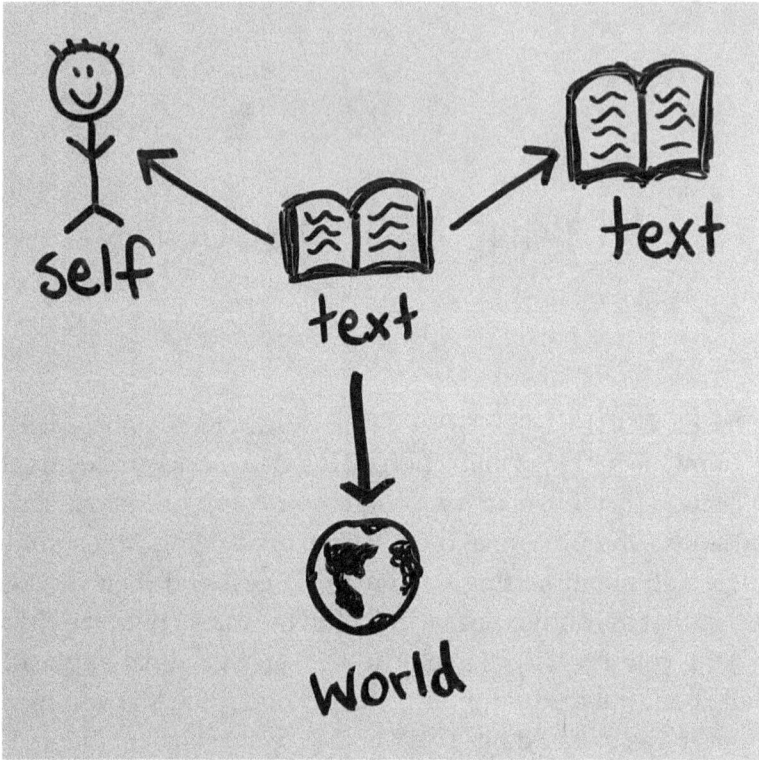

The three types of connections
Visit www.biblicalliteracyforkids.com to download this graphic.

For all types of connections, students can use this sentence frame to guide their thinking:

_____ reminds me of _____ because...

something from
the text

something
from my life
OR
another text
OR
something
from the
world

Text-to-Self Connections

A text-to-self connection happens when students bring together what is happening in the text with something from their personal lives. It is the easiest type of connection to make and the first one to model, but it also requires some guidance because students are prone to making unproductive connections when they are first learning the strategy. The difference between a productive and unproductive connection is this: **productive connections bring the reader a deeper understanding of the text, while unproductive connections distract from text comprehension.** For example, let's consider what might happen when students read Zephaniah 3:17:

> The Lord your God in your midst, The Mighty One, will save; He will rejoice over you with gladness, He will quiet you with His love, He will rejoice over you with singing. (NKJV)

Unproductive text-to-self connections will sound like this:

Student A: This passage talks about singing. I've sung before in my choir! We went on a trip and it was so much fun!

Student B: This passage says God is quiet. I always have to be quiet in class, and it's boring! (Notice that the passage says "He *will* quiet," not "He *is* quiet." So there are several things to correct in this example.)

Student C: This passage says God saves. That's just like what my T-shirt says: Jesus saves!

A productive text-to-self connection might sound like this:

Student D: This passage says that God will quiet us with His love. That reminds me of how my mom calms down my baby brother. She loves him and rocks him and helps him calm down.

Student D's connection is productive because it helps her understand more about God: she sees His character reflected in her mom's actions. But how can you teach students to make productive connections like Student D? Strong summarizing skills are needed to help readers distinguish between productive and unproductive connections. If you ground the discussion first by asking, "What is the most important part of this passage?", you can then follow up by making connections to important things, which keeps students on track. Let's look at how this might be done by using the passage from Zephaniah. That verse is packed with important details, but a summary might sound like this:

God is with us and saves us. We make him happy, and he helps us feel calm and safe.

It could also be simplified further to say:

This passage explains some ways that God takes care of us.

Either way, the summary makes it clear that God's care is the main focus of the passage. Let's see how we might address the comments of Students A, B, and C to get them back on track. First, let's examine how the adult might address Student A, who just wants to share about his choir trip:

Adult: Wow! It sounds like you had a really fun choir trip! But let's look again at our summary of the passage. Is it mostly about singing?

Student A: No.

Adult: I want to hear about your trip, but can you share it with me after our lesson?

Student A: Okay.

Adult: What was this passage mostly about?

Student A: Ummm…God caring for us?

Adult: Yes! Can you make a connection to that?

In this example, the adult makes an appointment with the student to hear what he really wants to share but uses the summary to guide the reader back on topic.

Now let's look at Student B, who misread the passage and then made an unproductive connection about being quiet:

Adult: Can you reread the phrase about being quiet?

Student B: Sure. *[Reading quickly]* … He is quiet you in His love.

Adult: Slow down and point to each word as you read. Try again.

Student B: *[Reading]* He is – oh wait! That says *will*. He *will* quiet you with His love.

Adult: Right. It doesn't say He *is* quiet but that He *will* quiet. What does it mean to quiet someone?

Student B: I don't know.

Adult: Think about a baby. Why would you need to quiet a baby?

Student B: Because it's crying and upset.

Adult: Right! *How* would you quiet it?

Student B: I could rock it or give it a blanket!

Adult: Great! Now this passage says that God will quiet *us* with His love. How might He do that? Can you make a connection?

In this exchange, the student's actual problem was with monitoring and clarifying because she didn't read the words correctly.

The adult guides her to fix the misunderstanding and then asks her to make a connection.

Now let's consider Student C, who is focused on his T-shirt.

> **Adult:** Yes, your T-shirt says, "Jesus saves." Why is it important that Jesus saves?
>
> **Student C:** Well, we need Jesus to save us from sin so we can be friends with Him.
>
> **Adult:** Right. Let's look back at the passage. Why is it important for God to save the people in this passage?
>
> **Student C:** Uh…
>
> **Adult:** Use our summary if you're stuck.
>
> **Student C:** Oh! Saving us is a way that God takes care of us!
>
> **Adult:** Right! Your T-shirt reminds us that Jesus saves us, which He does because He cares for us. That's the same reason God saves His people in this passage – because He cares for them.

The student in this example was the closest to making a productive connection, but he needed to focus less on his shirt and more on the *why* behind his shirt. The adult uses questioning to strengthen the student's connection, moving it from unproductive to productive. The adult might make a note of this student's response, "Saving us is a way that God takes care of us," so that the adult can come back to that idea in future discussions about personal application.

Text-to-self connections can be a powerful way for students to bring the truth of God's Word closer to their personal lives. For example, in this passage in Zephaniah, a student with anxiety, trauma, or even nightmares may really connect with the need for God's quieting love. Someone may have a story to share about how God has saved them or their family from a hard situation. Once students begin to make productive text-to-self connections, they start to see God's Word as personally relevant.

Text-to-Text Connections

The second type of connection is a text-to-text connection. **Text-to-text connections allow students to bring together the biblical passage they are reading with something else they have read.** When students connect the Bible to either a fiction or nonfiction text they have read, they begin to understand how God's Word is relevant to interpreting other sources of reading material. Readers can also connect one biblical passage to another, which is extremely helpful for understanding the biblical metanarrative, or the big, continuous story that God is telling throughout the whole Bible.

Let's look at Matthew 26:26-28 to see what text-to-text connections readers might find.

> While they were eating, Jesus took bread, and when he had given thanks, he broke it and gave it to his disciples, saying, "Take and eat; this is my body."
>
> Then he took a cup, and when he had given thanks, he gave it to them, saying, "Drink from it, all of you. This is my blood of the covenant, which is poured out for many for the forgiveness of sins.

Since Jesus is celebrating the Passover with his disciples, one of the best text-to-text connections would probably be to Exodus 12, where Moses is explaining the Passover celebration. It would be helpful to read Exodus 12 with your students and then explore some of the following questions to help your readers make connections:

- How was the first Passover similar to what Jesus is doing? (Don't forget to point out that Jesus is celebrating a Passover seder with his disciples.)

- How is Jesus' body like the bread used during the Passover? (This might require an additional text connection to understand, such as 1 Corinthians 5:6-8, where Paul compares yeast to sin. In Exodus 12, Moses explains that the Passover bread is to be unleavened. In Matthew 26, Jesus says that the bread is his body. After reading those two passages, and also the section in Corinthians, it becomes clearer why He would say that: His body is without sin.)

- How is the wine like Jesus' blood?

- How do these connections help us understand the passage better?

Text-to-text connections can add depth and richness to your conversations, but they require *a lot* of modeling at first because students are not used to viewing the Bible as a whole; rather, they tend to see it as a collection of stories that have nothing to do with each other. It is wise to find at least one text-to-text connection yourself as you prepare for your lesson so you can help guide students to make that type of connection. As they see more text-to-text connections modeled, readers will become more proficient at noticing them on their own.

Text-to-World Connections

The last type of connection, text-to-world, is key for teaching kids to have a biblical worldview. **A text-to-world connection happens when students bring together the passage they are reading with other world events, such as the news, history, scientific or archeological discoveries, or social media trends.** Many readers will not do this naturally at first, but once they see these types of connections to the world, they will see them everywhere! For any passage, a good starting place is to ask the students, "Does anything in this passage remind you of something from the news? School? Social media?" This type of questioning will help students bring the passage, which they may see as ancient and irrelevant, into the modern context in a meaningful way.

An interesting example of a text-to-world connection can be illustrated with Genesis 7. Verses 11 and 12 specifically explain how the flood happened:

> In the six hundredth year of Noah's life, on the seventeenth day of the second month — on that day all the springs of the great deep burst forth, and the floodgates of the heavens were opened. And rain fell on the earth forty days and forty nights.

When reading this, many students (and adults) may wonder, "What are the springs of the great deep?" They may also be curious about how water could possibly cover the whole earth if the water doesn't cover everything now. In other words, where did the water come from, and where did it go?

This is a great time to explain a text-to-world connection: recently, scientists have discovered a massive underground ocean over 400 miles below the Earth's surface. This underground water source contains three times the water of all the surface oceans combined! The lead geophysicist on the research team, Steven Jacobson, stated, "Without this internal water source, Earth's surface would likely be a barren landscape, with only mountain peaks peeking out from a vast ocean."[1]

In other words, the Earth would be completely covered in water if much of that water wasn't being stored underground. This is a wonderful text-to-world connection because it not only helps to explain how the flood happened, but it also reminds students that God's Word can be trusted. After all, the "springs of the great deep" have always been a part of the Genesis story, but scientists have only recently had the technology to prove their existence. Seeing plenty of text-to-world connections shows students why they can trust the Bible as their lens for viewing the world.

Remember that the ultimate goal of all biblical literacy training is for students to make sense of the text. With practice, students will automatically start making all sorts of connections as they read and discuss the Bible with others, which will provide them with insight into the relevance of God's Word in their everyday lives. Their connections will also be invaluable to them as they seek to understand the theme, lesson, and personal application of the passage, which will be detailed in the next chapter.

---

[1] The Weather Channel India Edit Team. April 4, 2024. "Massive Ocean Found 700 Kilometres Beneath Earth's Surface Changes What We Know About the Origins of Water!" Accessed June 19, 2024. https://weather.com/en-IN/india/science/news/2024-04-04-massive-ocean-found-700-kilometres-beneath-earth-surface.

8

Theme, Lesson, and Personal Application

THEME, LESSON, AND PERSONAL APPLICATION ARE THE fifth and sixth steps on the Reading Strategies Pyramid. These strategies are closely tied: once students understand the theme or lesson, it is nearly impossible to stop them from also seeing the personal application. Therefore, they are always taught together.

Theme or Lesson

The fifth step on the Reading Strategies Pyramid is called theme or lesson. **The lesson is an important teaching from a short biblical passage.** Every passage has a lesson. When you ask students, "What is this passage trying to teach me?", you're asking them to explain the lesson. **The theme is a big idea or main message that runs through a longer section of Scripture.** The theme is similar to a lesson, but not quite the same. Let's look at the story of Joseph from Genesis to illustrate the difference.

Joseph's story begins in Genesis 37 and continues for 12 chapters until the end of the book. In each chapter, students can discover several lessons. Of course, the lessons listed below are not the only lessons that can be gleaned from these chapters. The Bible is so rich that we can always find new insights if we keep studying it! Some example lessons might be:

Chapter	Example Lesson
37:1-11	God can speak to young people.
37:12-36	Jealousy leads to sin.
39	When you see temptation, run!
40	God gives people wisdom and insight.
41:1-40	God rewards people who are faithful to Him.
41:41-57	God uses His people to bless others.

When you ask students to tell you the lesson of a passage, you are focusing your discussion on a specific passage of scripture: a chapter or part of a chapter. In each teaching session with your students, they can find a lesson from that section of the Bible.

Finding the theme involves looking at larger chunks of the biblical text. In the example of Joseph's life, I would ask students about the theme of his whole story after we had thoroughly studied each of the 12 chapters about him. I would ask, "What can we learn from examining Joseph's whole life? What was God up to?"

What I really want students to do is make a bunch of text-to-text connections to see the larger story of his life and then summarize what they find. Joseph's life is a good one to use at first because he actually points out the theme of his life for us in Genesis 50:20: "You intended to harm me, but God intended it for good to accomplish what is now being done, the saving of many lives." So the theme would be that God will use all things, even evil things, for His good.

Finding the Lesson

When readers are looking for the lesson, they should ask themselves, "What can I learn from this story? What is the author trying to teach me?" Lessons can be positive (as in, "Do this!") or negative (as in, "Do not do this!"), but they are always instructive.

Let's listen to a conversation between an adult and a group of fifth-grade students after reading the story of Cain and Abel from Genesis chapter 4 to see how they go about finding the lesson in the text. Before this conversation, the group has already completed the steps of monitoring and clarifying, visualizing, summarizing, and making connections. Now they are ready to discover what the lesson might be.

> **Adult:** God included this story in the Bible for a reason. Why do you think it is in here? What lessons can it teach us?
>
> **Student A:** You should bring your best gifts to God.
>
> **Student B:** Sin affected everyone really fast, even though it hadn't been around very long.
>
> **Student C:** Anger can cause big problems.
>
> **Student D:** You should listen to God's warnings.
>
> **Student E:** Trying to hide your sin is never a good idea.
>
> **Adult:** Wow! These are all great lessons from the text. For our discussion, which one should we focus on?

Notice that the students pulled out many lessons from the text – and there are probably even more than that! The adult asked them to choose one to help focus the discussion, but he or she can always decide to return to this passage and examine another of its lessons at a later time. In this example, the group ultimately decided to choose Student C's "Anger can cause big problems" as the lesson they wanted to focus on since many members of the group had previously expressed difficulty in dealing with their own anger. Since finding the lesson leads up to the personal application discussion, this was a great choice.

Finding the Theme

As we discussed previously, theme is used for longer sections of scripture. Finding the theme is especially beneficial for passages from Psalms and Proverbs, which seem to be giving us a new lesson in each verse. Let's consider this example from Psalm 1:

1 Blessed is the one
   who does not walk in step with the wicked
or stand in the way that sinners take
   or sit in the company of mockers,
2 but whose delight is in the law of the Lord,
   and who meditates on his law day and night.
3 That person is like a tree planted by streams of water,
   which yields its fruit in season
and whose leaf does not wither—
   whatever they do prospers.
4 Not so the wicked!
   They are like chaff
   that the wind blows away.
5 Therefore the wicked will not stand in the judgment,
   nor sinners in the assembly of the righteous.
6 For the Lord watches over the way of the righteous,
   but the way of the wicked leads to destruction.

If I break down the Psalm by lessons, it might look something like this:

- Verses 1-2: Staying away from "the way of sinners" brings blessing.

- Verses 3 and 6a: The Lord watches over the righteous and brings them prosperity (good things).

- Verses 4-5 and 6b: The wicked will be destroyed.

In this case, none of these small lessons provide the best description of the whole Psalm, though they give readers clues about the theme. To find the theme, students need to ask, "What is the overarching idea from this whole text?" In the case of Psalm 1, the theme might sound like, "Being happy in following God's ways brings life and good things." Students can check to see if this theme matches the smaller lessons they found.

Personal Application

The last step on the Reading Strategies Pyramid is personal application. **In personal application, students explore how the lesson or theme affects their lives.** This is the step when readers realize that God's Word is actually speaking specifically *to them*.

The basic question to answer in personal application is: how can I apply this theme or lesson to my life? Because that question is so general, students often benefit from a more specific discussion. This series of questions might solicit better responses:

- How does the lesson/theme affect how I treat my family and friends?
- How does the lesson/theme change the way I work at home or at school?
- How does the lesson/theme change how I think of myself?
- How does the lesson/theme affect how I think about God?
- How does the lesson/theme change the way I think about the world?

Students may also benefit from using this graphic organizer:

This graphic organizer helps students think about all the ways the Bible can impact their personal lives.
Visit www.biblicalliteracyforkids.com to download this graphic.

Let's revisit the students' discussion of the Cain and Abel story. They decided that one of the important lessons in the passage was, "Anger can cause big problems." For personal application, the wording changes to, "Anger can cause big problems *for me.*" Then the students work out *how* anger can cause problems in their personal lives.

Below are two personal application examples that illustrate the point well. Student A, who was quite comfortable talking with the group, shared his personal application aloud. Student B is more reserved. She wrote her personal application in her Bible journal and shared it with the adult later:

> **Student A:** I get angry sometimes and lose my temper. I can treat other people pretty badly when I'm angry. I need to realize how I'm being tempted when I'm angry so I'm not like Cain.

> **Student B:** My mom has been very angry with God, kind of like how Cain was angry with God. I can see how that's not a great way to deal with things, and it seems to be hurting her relationship with God. When bad things happen, I think I need to pray to God about them without just getting mad.

Both of these students realized that the lesson in Genesis 4 affected their lives in very personal ways. They were able to explain what they learned from Cain's story and how they did not want to be like him. They were also willing to share their personal applications because they knew that they were in a safe place. The adult had done a wonderful job of cultivating relationships with her students using the strategies I shared in chapter two. During each lesson, even when they were just learning monitoring and clarifying, the adult modeled care, empathy, and support to her students. She appropriately shared how God has been working in her own life and how different passages applied to her. As a result, she reaped the reward of students who were willing to share deeply personal insights.

When a student shares a personal application like the ones above with you, make sure to pray for them. Depending on the setting, it might be appropriate for you to pull them aside after the lesson and pray right then. Also, be intentional about continuing to pray for them and check back with them to find out how things are going. Just like adults, students tend to have one or two areas in their lives that God is working on. For example, I would pray for Student

A to grow in patience. I would pray for Student B's relationship with her mom and her mom's relationship with God. Praying for students' growth in Christ is a powerful way to demonstrate His love and care for them.

Personal application is at the top of the Pyramid for a reason; getting it right depends on all of the strategies below it. But once your students get a taste for personal application, they will always want to know why the passage matters to their lives.

When students first begin learning this strategy, they need a lot of practice with passages that have obvious personal applications. Later, be prepared to push them to examine passages that require more effort to apply to their lives. Let's look at how to handle more difficult passages.

It's Always There if You Look

Have you ever noticed that the Bible insists that all Scripture is relevant – and even necessary – to our lives? As Paul instructs Timothy in 2 Timothy 3:16-17: "*All Scripture* is God-breathed and is useful for teaching, rebuking, correcting and training in righteousness, so that the servant of God may be thoroughly equipped for every good work" (emphasis mine). If these verses are really true, then what are we to do with highly technical books such as Leviticus or all of those genealogical records in 1 Chronicles? Since we are not living in Bible times, and we no longer worship God in the tabernacle, how can those passages actually be instructive to our lives?

These are excellent questions, and ones that your students will ask themselves as well. Students and adults need to understand that *personal application is always there if you look for it.* You may have to look hard, but one of the treasures of the Bible is that God is always saying something important through His Word. Another way to think about it is why would God bother to have these passages preserved for thousands of years if they were *not* important?

When I was teaching a group of sixth graders, I told them that every passage in the Bible has a personal application. Their response was, "Of course!" But then I asked them to turn to Leviticus 14:33-53, assuring them that they would find something valuable in the text. In my Bible, this section is titled "Cleansing From Defiling Molds." When they saw the passage, their faces told me two things: first, they were convinced that this passage had absolutely nothing to do with their lives; second, they were sure that their teacher had completely lost her mind. Still, I insisted that they read the passage anyway. And I would encourage you to do the same – grab your Bible and read those 20 verses.

When you read that passage, do you find it extremely helpful for your everyday life? If you're like my students, your answer would be an emphatic *no*. I asked them, "When was the last time you've had to deal with mold in your house? Do you even have houses made of stones and clay? Does God really think that this passage is important to us today?" My students were quite bewildered by my questions. Even so, we made a point to visualize and summarize the passage. Soon we had drawings of moldy houses, priests, worried people, and sacrificial birds all over the board.

Then my students got to see why text-to-text connections are so important: I had my students examine Peter 2:4-5, which says,

> As you come to him, the living Stone —rejected by humans but chosen by God and precious to him — you also, like living stones, are being built into a spiritual house to be a holy priesthood, offering spiritual sacrifices acceptable to God through Jesus Christ.

We discussed how this passage is written to believers who are being compared to living stones in a house. My students quickly noticed that this "house" sounded much like the houses mentioned in Leviticus. I also reminded them that 1 Corinthians 6:19 says that we are "temples of the Holy Spirit," which is essentially "God's house." So we are compared to a house more than once in the biblical text. Then I asked them, "If we are like the house, then what could the mold represent?" It didn't take long until someone shouted, "Sin! The mold is like sin!"

We examined the passage closely to see if the mold really was like sin. We saw that priests were commanded to take the spreading of the mold quite seriously, just as we are told to take our sin seriously. If the mold kept spreading, the stones of the house were to be removed and cast out into an unclean place. This reminded my students of another text-to-text connection: Jesus' words in Mark 9 about removing your hand, foot, or eye if it causes you to sin. Finally, the mold had to be atoned for through a blood sacrifice, just as sin required the death of Jesus.

I told them, "This passage isn't just about mold. It's also a picture of Jesus. You are like the house. Jesus wants to come in and remove your old, sinful way of life and make you new, just as the priests had to replace the contaminated stones and plaster. Like the birds, He is the sacrifice that makes us pure in God's sight."

My students never looked at obscure Bible passages the same way after that. As we continued to work through hard texts together, they began to understand that the whole Bible has something to say to them. Sometimes the personal application might not be obvious, and sometimes they had to read more of a passage's context to see it, but the application was always there.

Ask the Hard Questions

When students move from being children to adolescents, they begin to ask hard questions about themselves, the world, and their faith. If, as multiple proverbs state, the fear of the Lord is the beginning of wisdom and knowledge, then teaching students to take their questions to the Lord and His Word should be an important part of biblical literacy instruction. Once older students are well-versed in personal application, they are also ready to use this strategy to begin tackling hard questions about the Bible with guidance and prompting from you.

For example, I was once studying Exodus with a group of fifth graders. We had just finished reading Genesis, so my readers had great background knowledge for Exodus. They were also well-practiced in using the skills on the Reading Strategies Pyramid, so they were ready for me to push them more in the area of personal application and in answering hard questions.

The first chapter of Exodus is packed with terrible things: the Israelites go from being blessed in the land of Egypt to a life of slavery, they are treated ruthlessly, and Pharaoh gives orders for all of the baby Hebrew boys to be thrown into the Nile to die a horrible death. After we read this passage, my students had almost no reaction to what they had read. Since the passage was familiar to them, they weren't really thinking about it much. So we summarized the terrible things that had happened, and I wrote them on the board.

Then I turned to them and asked, "How could God let this happen? I thought He was a good God! Isn't He in control of everything?" My students replied that yes, of course God was in control of everything. So I pressed them further, "If He's really in control, then what is He doing? Why is He letting His people suffer? Why is He letting all of these babies die? He is letting bad things happen! Why?!"

My students were absolutely stunned. For one thing, they had never thought of these questions before. But what disturbed them the most was that they didn't have an answer. They could not explain why a loving God would allow His people to suffer. Some of them attempted pat answers, such as, "It's just part of His plan." But I pushed them by asking, "How would you feel if your baby brother was killed and God did nothing about it? He *could* do something, but He *didn't*. Would you be okay with that?"

At that point, they suddenly found that they didn't have any good answers anymore. What was even more frustrating for them was that I also refused to give them an answer during that session. I didn't even give them an answer during the next session – just more seemingly unanswerable questions! I told them that they would be discovering the answers as we read Exodus together and that they would need all of their biblical literacy skills to figure them out.

It's important to note that I did not ask them these questions to shake their faith; rather, I asked them these questions to help fortify their faith. I know that one day they will likely face suffering and question God's goodness. I also know that we live in a time of religious deconstruction, when it is popular for people to completely disassemble the faith they once held so that they no longer believe it anymore. So I wanted to model the process of struggling with hard questions in a safe environment; I was there with them to keep them on track and guide them back to the truth. I wanted to show them that it is okay to question things and that the safest place to take those questions is to God and His Word.

Throughout our reading of Exodus, students made insightful connections to the Book of Job, the suffering of Jesus, and their own personal struggles. Ultimately, they discovered that we will not always understand God and His ways – that is why He is God and we are not. However, they also realized that God was glorified through the struggles of His people and His deliverance of them, which drew more people to Himself. They were reminded of what they had learned from reading Genesis, which is that the point of life is to know and love our Creator, and Exodus showed them how difficulty can help people know Him better. Most importantly, they found that they could ask hard questions and, with perseverance, find the answers to them in the biblical text.

When your students show readiness to handle mature subjects and struggle with ideas, asking these types of hard questions is imperative. If you don't, the world will; how much better it will be for those students who are prepared to seek God when they don't know the answers.

In the next chapter, we will see how to put all of these strategies together to plan appropriate lessons.

9

Putting It All Together

THROUGHOUT THIS BOOK, MY GOAL HAS BEEN TO DE-
scribe each step of the Reading Strategies Pyramid in enough
detail that you can use each one with confidence. But how can
you put all of these strategies together to plan a lesson? How can
you get through so many strategies at once? What does a complete
lesson look like? Let's find out the answers to these questions and
examine the appropriate steps for putting everything together.

Writing to Learn

Many strategies in the Reading Strategies Pyramid ask students to
write to show their thinking. This is intentional, but know that it is
not a forever expectation. While they are learning the strategies,
readers are processing a lot of new information. A written record of
their thinking prevents them from getting lost and allows the adult
to quickly assess their understanding. Writing also forces students
to organize their thoughts coherently.

However, the goal is *not* to have readers write paragraphs about
every passage they read. Once students have mastered a skill, writing about it can become optional if you wish. Even visualizing,
which involves drawing at first, is not necessary to record every time
unless it is beneficial. The best time to make writing optional for a
skill is after it's been in the students' responsibility column for a
while and they have demonstrated proficiency. Before that, the writing requirement will usually aid your discussion.

Can They Replicate Your Materials?

Maximizing the benefits of biblical literacy instruction means you must use materials that students will be able to find and use on their own. In other words, it's important to ask yourself, "Would my students be able to use these materials if I wasn't here with them?" While some adults like to use cute worksheets or graphic organizers for instruction, these are unhelpful for students in the long run if they are used for every lesson. The goal of biblical literacy instruction is to empower students to read and understand the Bible on their own. So, they need to be confident in their ability to replicate supportive materials as they need them. Instead of giving readers a printout, give them a piece of paper. Use sticky notes, blank pages, or lined paper – things that they will be able to easily acquire on their own. Keeping your materials *simple* and *portable* will greatly benefit your students, especially when they are attempting to use these skills independently outside of instructional time.

Creating Lessons

As you plan, consider where your students are in the process of learning biblical literacy strategies. If they are beginners, they are going to spend quite a bit of time with the strategies at the base of the Pyramid until they master them. If they have learned more strategies, they will spend more time discussing the theme, lesson, and personal application. Let's revisit the Cain and Abel story from Genesis 4 so we can see how this lesson might look with different groups of students.

Beginner Lesson Outline

These students are still learning monitoring, clarifying, and visualizing.

1. Read the passage together.

2. Spend most of the discussion time on monitoring and clarifying to determine what the passage means. Teach dictionary or Bible handbook use as appropriate.

3. Ask students to draw what happened (visualizing).

4. Say, "This story is about how Cain was so angry that he killed his brother. He didn't take care of his first sin against God, so that caused an even bigger problem. I know I sometimes treat people badly when I'm angry, so this story reminds me to take care of my anger right away."

Notice that the adult summarizes for the students at this stage. She also explains the lesson and personal application, but she doesn't go into great detail or invite much discussion about them. This is because the adult recognizes that the students have expended most of their mental energy on strategies to just understand the text. Her explanation at the end shows them that there is more to the passage than what they have discussed, but she does not overwhelm them by expecting them to also do the higher strategies.

Intermediate Lesson Outline

These students are confident in their ability to monitor, clarify, and visualize. Now these students need to focus on summarizing and/or making connections.

1. Read the passage together.

2. Give students time to draw what happened in the story. At this point, you expect them to use the dictionaries or other resources and to ask clarifying questions as needed.

3. Have them share their drawings and tell you what happened in the story so that you can check for monitoring and clarifying problems.

4. Spend most of your discussion time on summarizing and making connections.

5. Say, "Cain didn't take care of his sin and anger, which caused some pretty bad consequences. This reminds me of how I need to deal with my anger right away so it doesn't cause problems in my life."

Notice that the adult has completely handed off monitoring, clarifying, and visualizing responsibilities and will only revisit those skills to fix problems. She explains the lesson and personal application at the end but still isn't inviting much discussion about those.

Advanced Lesson Outline

These students can confidently monitor, clarify, visualize, summarize, and make connections. Now they need to focus on theme, lesson, and personal application.

1. Read the passage together.
2. Ask the students to summarize what's happened.
3. Ask, "Does anyone have a connection to this passage?"
4. Spend most of your discussion time on theme, lesson, and personal application.

Notice that visualizing has been completely dropped in this example; the adult is confident that the students are doing this strategy mentally, so she left it out for the sake of time. In fact, she skipped straight to summarizing and would only need to revisit the lower strategies if there is a problem. This approach gives you more time for an in-depth discussion of the higher strategies, and moves your lessons to covering larger portions of the Bible, without wearing out your readers.

Here is an example of a lesson plan I created for a passage in Mark. This one is just meant to be used as an example, so it is more detailed, but you do not need to plan in this much detail for your own lesson. You can find detailed lesson plans like these for specific books of the Bible on my website at www.biblicalliteracyforkids.com.

Mark 1:21-28 – Jesus Drives Out an Evil Spirit
Suggested timeframe: 1 session

Modeling and Handing Off

Use this chart to decide how to structure your lesson.

Student Responsibility	Students and Adults Together	Adult Modeling
These are strategies the students have learned so well that they no longer need your help.	This is where you will spend the bulk of your lesson. Most of your discussion will revolve around learning this strategy.	These are strategies that you will briefly mention so that students know they exist, but you will not be teaching them to students.
Check all that apply.	**Check ONE.**	**Check all that apply.**
☐ Monitoring & Clarifying AND Visualizing ☐ Summarizing ☐ Making Connections ☐ Theme or Lesson	☐ Monitoring & Clarifying AND Visualizing ☐ Summarizing ☐ Making Connections ☐ Theme or Lesson ☐ Personal Application	☐ Summarizing ☐ Making Connections ☐ Theme or Lesson ☐ Personal Application

Monitoring and Clarifying

Ask your students about words, phrases, and concepts that you think might be confusing. Depending on their age, here are some things that might get in the way of students' comprehension:

Vocabulary Words & Phrases	Background Knowledge
• Sabbath • Synagogue • Authority	• Students need to understand a little about who the teachers of the law were, why they were teaching "the law," and why they are in the synagogue. • When kids today think of the law, they think of things like, "Don't text and drive." So you need to clarify for them that the passage is talking about the Law of Moses and the Jewish tradition, which were religious laws that every Jew had to follow.

Monitoring & Clarifying Questions:

- Why would Jesus have more authority than the teachers of the law? (Because He is God's Son, and God is the ultimate authority)
- How did Jesus show that He has authority? (By driving out the evil spirit).

Visualizing

Students should draw what is happening in the passage. You might want to show them a picture of a synagogue if you have one.

Summarizing

Work with your students to make a good summary.

Example: Jesus showed His authority by commanding an evil spirit to come out of a man. It immediately came out!

Making Connections

If your students are stuck, these questions might help:

- Where else in the Bible do we see that God (or Jesus) has authority over evil?
- This reminds me of (Star Wars, Marvel, etc.) when _____ (character) was fighting evil. But that character didn't have authority like Jesus because…
- Who is someone you know who has authority over something? How do you know that they have authority? (Parents, pastors, teachers, coaches, police officers, etc. are all great examples.)

Theme or Lesson

Listen to your students to see if they can pull out a theme or lesson. Students should be able to use evidence from the text to back up their theme or lesson. Remember that there is often more than one theme or lesson in any given passage.

Examples:

- **Jesus has authority over evil.**
- **Evil is not in charge; Jesus is!** (This type of summary might be easier for younger kids who are just learning the concept of "authority.")

Personal Application

Each student's personal application should be directly related to one of the themes or lessons.

Example:

I don't have to be afraid of _____ (evil thing) because Jesus has power and authority over it. (You might ask, "How does knowing Jesus has authority over evil change the way you pray about it?")

Let the Holy Spirit Interrupt

Keep in mind that the Holy Spirit is very concerned with your students' growth – even more than you are. Because He knows the hearts and minds of your readers intimately, He will prompt them to make connections or personal applications that are *not* in your plans but are very relevant to His plans. This type of interruption has happened to me more times than I can count, and I have never been sorry when I followed His lead in the discussion.

In fact, I would say that those lessons have been the most rich and formative for the spiritual growth of my students. I have even had several students make personal decisions to follow Jesus when I decided to follow the Holy Spirit instead of what was on my lesson plan. So prepare for the discussion and make plans, but don't fight the divine interruptions when they come.

The Lord Is Your Strength

As we close out our time together, remember that God is ultimately the one in charge of this whole process. Lean on Him and His strength and He will grant you wisdom as you work with your students. Pray and ask for insights and He will grant them to you. Entrust your students' growth to Him, remain faithful and patient, and then watch as He transforms your readers through the power of His Word.

Afterword

After Joshua had dismissed the Israelites, they went to take possession of the land, each to their own inheritance. The people served the LORD throughout the lifetime of Joshua and of the elders who outlived him and who had seen all the great things the LORD had done for Israel…
After that whole generation had been gathered to their ancestors, another generation grew up who knew neither the LORD nor what he had done for Israel. Then the Israelites did evil in the eyes of the LORD and served the Baals. They forsook the LORD, the God of their ancestors, who had brought them out of Egypt. They followed and worshiped various gods of the peoples around them. They aroused the LORD's anger because they forsook him and served Baal and the Ashtoreths.

– Judges 2:6-7, 10-13 (NIV)

ANYONE WHO HAS EVER READ JUDGES CAN TESTIFY THAT it is a frustrating book to read. Over and over again, the Israelites sin, endure God's punishment, cry out to God, experience His deliverance, and…repeat the cycle again. The beginning of Judges points out that the people did take possession of the promised land, but they still failed to remain faithful to God. Why? Judges 2:10 gives us a clue: "Another generation grew up who knew neither the LORD nor what he had done for Israel." How could this have possibly happened? Simply, the adults failed to pass on their knowledge of God and His ways to the children.

It's not like the Israelite adults didn't know what to do. Deuteronomy chapter 11 is full of instructions about loving and obeying the Lord, but in verses 18-21, God specifically charges the parents with certain tasks:

> Fix these words of mine in your hearts and minds; tie them as symbols on your hands and bind them on your foreheads. Teach them to your children, talking about them when you sit at home and when you walk along the road, when you lie down and when you get up. Write them on the doorframes of your houses and on your gates, so that your days and the days of your children may be many in the land the LORD swore to give your ancestors, as many as the days that the heavens are above the earth.

God instructed the parents to intentionally bring up their children in the faith. He knew that both the children and parents needed verbal and written reminders of His law, and He was supposed to be a constant topic of discussion among His people. Those families in Judges failed in their responsibility to pass on their faith, bringing disastrous consequences to their children and to their nation as a whole.

The world wants your children's allegiance. Society insists there are multiple religious paths, many ways to God, and numerous ways to be considered "righteous." It abhors single-minded focus on the one true God. Like the Israelites of old, we face a choice: will we pass on our faith? Will we be diligent in teaching the children even when we are busy? Even when we are tired? Even when life is hard? Even when the teaching seems difficult or tedious?

Adults can positively impact a child's faith more than they realize. When writing to Timothy, the apostle Paul remarked, "I am reminded of your sincere faith, which first lived in your grandmother Lois and in your mother Eunice and, I am persuaded, now lives in you also" (2 Tim. 1:5). Timothy's role models set him up for success, providing him with the foundation he needed to fulfill God's calling on his life. When we pass on the gift of biblical literacy, we are similarly arming the children in our lives with a sound biblical worldview, a growing faith in God, and the spiritual survival skills they need to thrive in these dark days.

In Daniel 12:3, the prophet wrote, "Those who are wise will shine like the brightness of the heavens, and those who lead many to righteousness, like the stars for ever and ever." May you be that bright star for your students, leading them ever closer to Jesus and the life that only He can give.

References

Barna Group. 2022. "Explore the Data." Accessed September 30, 2024. https://www.barna.com/the-open-generation/explore-the-data/.

Barna Group. October 5, 2022. "Global Teens Share Their Perceptions of Jesus, the Bible & Justice." Accessed September 30, 2024. https://www.barna.com/research/open-generation-perceptions/.

Christianbook. "Translation Reading Levels." Accessed June 20, 2025. https://www.christianbook.com/page/bibles/about-bibles/bible-translation-reading-levels.

Hartman, Nick. October 26, 2022. "A Reflection on Barna's Open Generation Report." Accessed September 30, 2024. https://www.youthpastortheologian.com/blog/a-reflection-on-barnas-open-generation-report.

The Weather Channel India Edit Team. April 4, 2024. "Massive Ocean Found 700 Kilometres Beneath Earth's Surface Changes What We Know About the Origins of Water!" Accessed June 19, 2024. https://weather.com/en-IN/india/science/news/2024-04-04-massive-ocean-found-700-kilometres-beneath-earth-surface.

U.S. Department of Education. 2022 Reading Assessment. Institute of Education Sciences, National Center for Education Statistics, National Assessment of Educational Progress (NAEP).

www.ingramcontent.com/pod-product-compliance
Lightning Source LLC
La Vergne TN
LVHW052035080426
835513LV00018B/2338